Birth

Where Culture and Medicine Meet

The Pierre Vellay Portfolio

Martha Deed, PhD

Acknowledgments

Journal entries first appeared in Friendly Woman. Summer 1977. Pp 4-5.
All names have been changed except for Dr. Vellay.

All photographs unless otherwise credited: Martha Deed
Documents and photograph p 5: Martha Deed and Deed Family Papers

Author's portrait, p 38: Tara Bazilian-Chang, Photographer.

Photos of Dr. Vellay's Maison de Verre interior and exterior views were obtained under Common License: (https://en.wikipedia.org/wiki/Maison_de_Verre).

Screenshots of Dr. Vellay videos: https://www.youtube.com/watch?v=xTF_Uk8qXzk

Street view of 31, rue St-Guillaume obtained from Google Maps.

Page decorations (fleurons) are taken from *Bulletin Officiel de la Société Internationale de Psycho-Prophylaxie Obstétricale. Octobre-Décembre 1971 and Juillet 1973-Mars 1974 No Special.*

Dr. Deed is particularly grateful to the late Dr. Pierre Vellay for his generosity and access to his childbirth education class, to his patients, and to the staff at his maternity clinique.

Thanks, too, to the dozens of women who offered their experiences and wisdom through dozens of interviews from 1973 – 1979.

Additional thanks to the women who gave me permission to use photographs of them and their babies.

Front and back cover design: Martha Deed
Front and back cover photographs: Martha Deed

Friends of Spork
Buffalo, New York USA
ISBN-13: 978-1974326778
ISBN-10:1974326772

The Riddle of the Research

This story is not straight. It bends around blind curves. Sometimes it drops into a crevice. It follows principles of social science, but ventures into untidy swamps. This is because humans are involved.

```
    May 1973
    . . . . Tonight, I am walking in the hall, practic-
ing so that I can go home tomorrow with three-day
old Anna.  I meet a Black father in
his green paper gown, rolling his baby back to the
nursery.
    "What did you have?" he asks.
    "A girl."
    "I had one, too, " he says. "Well--congratula-
tions anyway."
                    *   *   *



    July, 1973

    Every mother I meet seems to be overwhelmed by
one--and only one--aspect of taking care of a baby.
Mary can't stand her baby's not eating. Linda still
vomits once in awhile when she encounters a generous
b.m.   For me, it's sleep--and the lack thereof.
    Mind-destroying, bone-aching fatigue can strike
at any time, depends upon Anna's sleep and
willingness to entertain herself in the morning.
    Joy is marred by too many meals eaten against the
background of insistent wailing.  It is not an emer-
gency, I protest.  Let me swallow my food first
--please.
    I leave the table not knowing how much I have
eaten--or whether it tasted good.  Even my stomach
is confused by the noise and the tension.
                    *   *   *
```

Not the beginning. After the beginning.

Points of Departure.

Not a Hudson River Dayliner, but a voyage that requires a passport.

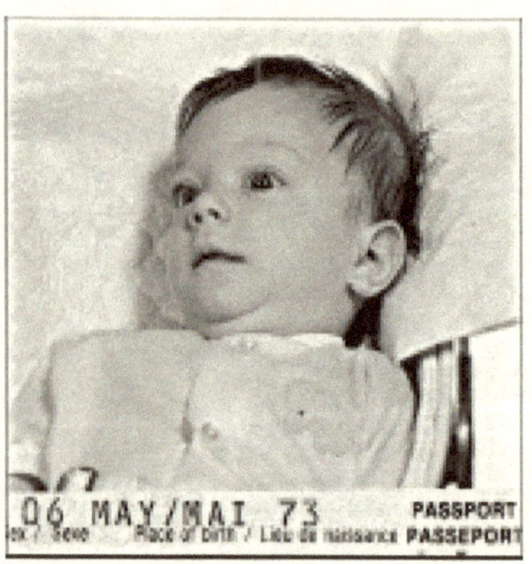

Like this. But where is the research element?

The future researcher knew of the request her great grandmother had made to her uncle during World War 2 when he was dispatched to France to fight the Nazis, but her great grandmother thought the greater duty was for him to go there to find her husband's relatives.

The mother who sat on the deck of the *France* in July 1973 carried with her a copy of those notes although the likelihood of finding these relatives was now less than probable.

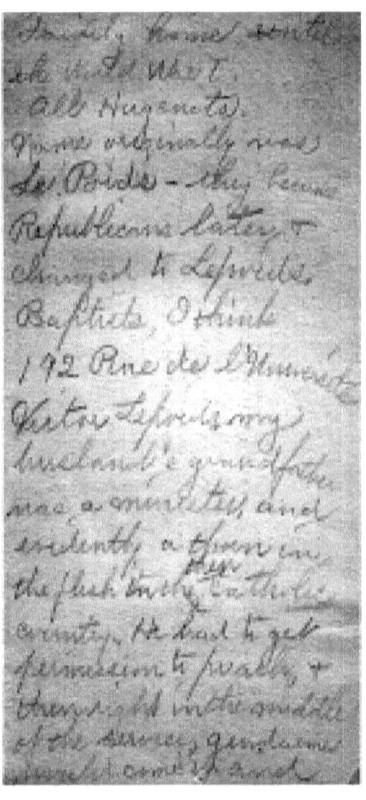

Family home before
the World War I
All Huguenots.
Family originally was
LePoids — they became
Republicans later &
changed to Lepoids
Baptists, I think
192 Rue de l'Universite
Victor Lepoids my
husband's grandfather
was a minister and
evidently a thorn in
the flesh with the Catholic
country. He had to get
permission to preach &
then right in the middle
of the service, gendarmes
would come and
[arrest him.]

It could be argued that they were going home.

There were even a birth certificate and an affidavit to prove a French connection to the researcher with seals and stamps and extracts of the relevant laws – and signatures of the attestor and his witnesses and the several notaries of the jurisdictions it passed through.

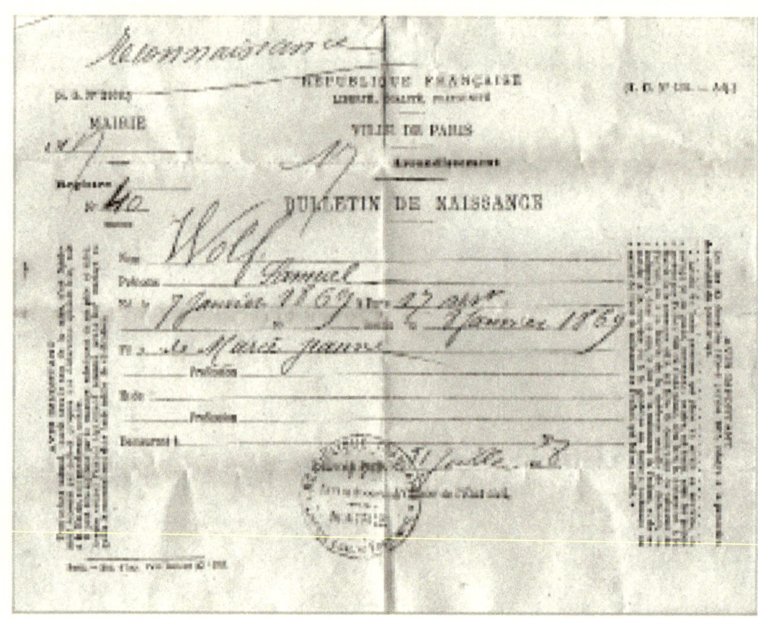

A birth certificate with more than a hint of scandal. The French ancestor was born out of wedlock in 1869. Paternity was not acknowledged by his father until 1888 when the father offered a separate "Narrative of Birth" at the prefecture in the jurisdiction where the ancestor was born.

These facts were not known to the researcher until she translated the documents decades later. Even then, the discovery of the birth certificate and its meaning was merely of family significance. It shed no light on the researcher's motivation for undertaking her project.

Motivations may be found inside a gray folder marked "Vellay" along with reprints of the 1970's and 1980's publications discovered in a box in the bottom of a rarely visited closet in a house in upstate New York in 2017, although it must also be said that these combinations of geography grow increasingly challenging to the reader's credulity.

December, 1976

    Where does the sense of <u>damage</u>
originate that is so much a part
of being female? For weeks, my
mind has circled around this
thought, and I've vowed to explore
it.
    Was my perception of my mother,
in itself, evidence of the deval-
uation I felt in being female?
                *   *   *

    May, 1977

    A group of women, many of them
Quakers, are sitting in a room
describing their mothers.
    "Of course, I hated my mother,
too," says the ninth or tenth
speaker to general, rueful laugh-
ter.
    I listen to the crimes of
mothers against daughters. (I
have had similar experiences my-
self.) I compare the mothers'
behavior with my own in the con-
text of intense tenderness toward
the small person who emerged from my
body, is formed like me, but who
is determinedly, unalterably, not
me, even at the age of three.
    Will she be sitting in a group
like this ten years, twenty or
thirty years from now -- hating <u>me</u>?
                *   *   *

The researcher's new mother journal brings us closer, but there is still the matter of the researcher's parents' flower girl to pull it all together. . .

When the researcher told her parents she was moving to France to take a job — later found not to exist and so leaving the researcher at loose ends in a country where she barely spoke the language upon arrival — her mother said:

"You must look up our flower girl. She lives in Paris."

The suggestion did not "take" in the midst of finding housing and grocery stores and sandboxes and doctors.

The non-existent job exposed for what it was, the New York apartment sublet to feminists for the year, the researcher took to the sandboxes where she began hearing women's stories of childbirth in Paris and elsewhere.

She began asking permission to tell those stories. The playground women were eager to share those stories.

And then — suddenly the researcher's baby was a year old and in need of a "Made in USA" kiddie car — the researcher's parents arrived for a visit, carrying the kiddie car under one arm, along with umbrellas, binoculars and suitcases.

Only then did the researcher learn that her apartment was a mere street or two away from the flower girl's home. The researcher and her mother met the flower girl at her house for afternoon *gouter*.

The turn comes here.

The flower girl was well acquainted with one of the most prominent obstetricians anywhere. He was the heir apparent of the Lamaze childbirth method, and his home office could almost be seen from the window of the flower girl's *troisième étage* (fourth floor to North Americans, because the French first floor is the American's second floor) apartment.

6

His home office, in fact, was itself significant enough to merit (decades later) its own Wikipedia page.

Not because of the street side *façade* and *porte cochère* (entrance) to 31, rue St.-Guillaume,

but because — inside that gate one finds the *Maison de Verre* (Glass House), designed by Pierre Chareau and Bernard Bijvoet.

The house was revolutionary in its day (constructed 1929 – 1932), and is still recognized as a significant example of modern architecture, incorporating industrial elements – metal pipes, glass block walls, rubber tile floors – into a private residence. The original owner of the house was himself a doctor and a political revolutionary. In 1974, the son-in-law of the original owner was also a doctor and a revolutionary as well – as a leading proponent of *Accouchement sans Douleur* (ASD) or Painless Childbirth.

The owner of the Glass House in 1974 was Dr. Pierre Vellay. Dr. Vellay had accompanied Dr. Fernand Lamaze on his trips to Russia where he had encountered childbirth methods unknown in Western Europe. After Lamaze's death, Dr. Vellay had carried on their work.

Somehow – the circumstances remain unknown – Dr. Vellay and the flower girl had met. Now the flower girl offered to introduce the researcher to Dr. Vellay.

3, rue de Grenelle
75006-Paris

July 19,1974

Dr. Pierre Vellay
31, rue Saint Guillaume
75007-Paris

Dear Dr. Vellay:

I am a licensed psychologist from New York State (USA), and I am currently living in Paris while writing a book on the psychological aspects of pregnancy and childbirth.

I would like very much to attend the series of preparation for childbirth classes given through your office. This would help me to make comparisons between maternity care practices in the United States and France. My husband and I attended the full set of classes at Women's Hospital (St. Luke's Medical Center, New York City) last year while preparing for the birth of our daughter. These classes were based largely on the French approach, but adapted for American women. Also, as part of my study, I have read <u>Childbirth Without Pain</u> (in English) and your chapter in Howells' <u>Modern Perspectives in Psycho-Obstetrics</u>.

At present, I read and understand spoken French quite well, but my ability to speak and write French is still quite limited. I have not been able to conduct interviews in French as yet, but I understand enough to follow classes in French.

Please feel free to respond in French. If you wish to meet me or to have one of your associates do so before answering my request, I would happy to make an appointment.

Sincerely,

Martha L. Deed, Ph.D.
Licensed Psychologist

From here, the road runs almost straight. The letter was answered on the day it was written and received.

Paris, le 19 Juillet 1974;

Madame Martha L. Deed,
3, rue de Grenelle

75006 - PARIS

Chère Madame,

     Avant de s'absenter de Paris jusqu'au 29 Juillet, le Docteur VELLAY me charge de répondre à votre lettre du 19.

     Il est, naturellement, tout à fait d'accord pour vous rencontrer et vous permettre d'assister à des cours de préparation à l'A.S.D., théoriques et pratiques, mais nous sommes en pleine période de congés annuels et notre équipe de monitrices n'est plus au complet.

     Vous pourrez appeler le Docteur VELLAY dès le début Août, de façon à voir avec lui ce qui peut être prévu pour vous faciliter les choses.

     En attendant,

     Nous vous prions de croire, chère Madame, en l'assurance de nos sentiments les meilleurs.

Secrétaire du
Docteur Pierre VELLAY.

The researcher — true to her claims — understood the letter, and the appointment was set for August 10th at 6 PM.

By then, she had already attended the first class in Dr. Vellay's childbirth course. Her French was no longer as rudimentary as it had been upon arrival in Paris a year earlier. She translated his lecture spontaneously into English notes.

<u>Translation</u>

DOCTOR PIERRE VELLAY
gynecologist-Obstetrician   Paris, July 19, 1974;

———

31, RUE ST-GUILLAUME
        PARIS (VIITH)
    TEL. : 548-59-93   Mrs. Martha Deed,
                                                  3, rue de Grenelle
———   75006 – <u>PARIS</u>

            Dear Madame,

        Since he will be away until July 29th, Dr. Vellay has asked
me to respond to your letter of the 19th.

        Of course, he is completely willing to meet you and to allow you to
attend his classes in preparation of ASD theory and practice, but we are in our
annual vacation period and out staff of assistants is incomplete.

        If you would telephone Dr. Vellay about the beginning of August, we
will be able to make arrangements for the class and a meeting.

        Meanwhile,

        We ask you to believe, dear Madame, in the assurance of
our best wishes.

                Secretary of
                Docteur Pierre VELLAY
                    //signature//

——— ● ———

The Research

The salon in the *Maison de Verre* served as the classroom for Dr. Vellay's childbirth education classes.

Dr. Pierre Vellay in lecture mode. Images taken from videos made before he moved into his glass house.

Pierre Vellay   Accouchement sans Douleur   August 2, 1974

1 – Education – get rid of what you know

      learn that pregnancy is normal

      avoid "psychological pollution"

e.g. "If you cross your legs, you'll cut the cord."

      not pathological sickness

      it's physiological

2 – "apprentissage"

      practicing for giving birth

12 years ago began ASD with Lamaze

1 – not enough to go to class & stay in bed all day

      have to make and effort to learn

          to practice

          to be successful on birth day

2 –Birth goes better even with difficulties if you're prepared.

3 – World is not well-educated – each time you speak of pregnancy

      <u>watch out</u>.   People will be very aggressive with you.

The better you know pregnancy, the more you're aware of difficulties –

. . . the better you'll do.

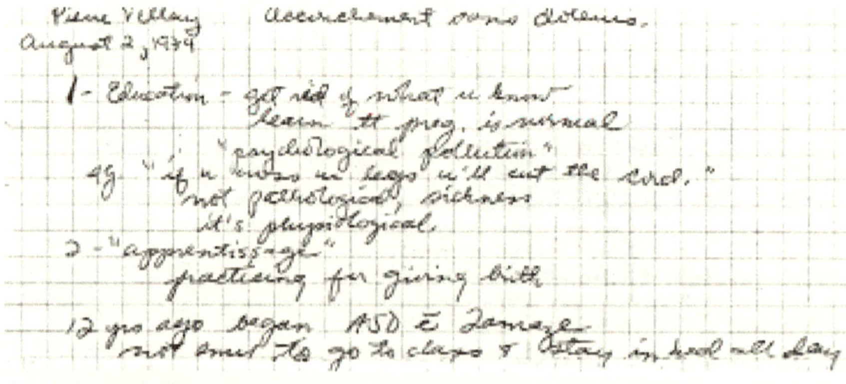

Note French quadrille paper.

At a meeting between Dr. Pierre Vellay and the researcher, August 10, 1974 —

Dr. Vellay offered to give the researcher names of his American patients whose babies he had delivered in the past year.

After the course was finished, the researcher would be free to invite participants in the course to be interviewed before and after delivery to see how the education and childbirth methods were working and to see if there were issues that should be addressed.

The researcher would meet with Dr. Vellay after the interviews were completed to report the results to him.

The researcher and Dr. Vellay agreed that they would not discuss the interviews until they were completed and that Dr. Vellay would not learn which of his patients had participated in the study. This would prevent contamination of the research — staff altering behavior due to knowledge that a patient's experience would be reported back to Dr. Vellay or Dr. Vellay influenced by knowledge that a patient was reporting her experiences to the researcher.

And here the essentially straight road made a slight, but significant turn. The sandbox interviews were unstructured, spontaneous, and followed no set protocol. They were more like stories one would hear over the back fence or read in a newspaper than pieces of scientific research.

In essence, they were journalism, not social science. If the researcher intended to accept Dr. Vellay's offers, she would need to move to a more rigorous set of constraints for the interviews.

———— ● ————

<u>The Setting</u>

On rue St Guillaume on Paris's Left Bank, there is a glass house in the courtyard of an old building. To enter, a visitor much choose one of three bells: *"Docteur," "Visites,"* or *"Service."* A patient approaching the door for the first time may not know which bell to ring and may be put off initially by the cold fading elegance of the interior as well, which is alleviated by sunlight streaming into an unusually large private garden equipped with swings and a slide along with conventional, formal plantings.

Dr. Pierre Vellay's office overlooks his garden, but he pays little attention to it, swiveling in his chair to face his patient across a cluttered desk unexpectedly stacked high with drug samples, Nembutol prominent among them, in brightly colored boxes. The office is large, lined with well-filled bookcases, and well-appointed with carpeting, a mixture of style and chrome furniture and by brass lamps, but dimly lit. His examining room opens off to the right. The man himself is imposing at first, handsome, vigorous, unexpectedly youthful, an air of sensuality in his manner.

People whose knowledge of obstetrics is current may recognize Pierre Vellay as an associate of Fernand Lamaze who brought *"accouchement sans douleur"* (ASD) to France in the early 1950s. Indeed, many of the women Vellay sees have read his books previously. *Childbirth without Pain*, published in 1959 (with co-authors Aline Vellay, Colette Jeanson, Andre Bourrel, Micheline Bourrel with Denise Lloyd, translator for the U.S. edition published by Dutton) is still widely read by women contemplating "natural" or "prepared" childbirth.

In the office, they encounter a complex man, whose sincerity and commitment to what he calls "childbirth without pain" is unmistakable, and who is unexpectedly personal in his physical examinations. Some of his American patients declare him a male chauvinist even as they appreciate his help to experience childbirth free of fear or trauma, and rich in significance for them and their attending husbands.

Complicated, surprising, inconsistent are all adjectives that women from the United States might apply to this prominent obstetrician, who is considered Lamaze's successor and a leading proponent of ASD or the Psycho-prophylactic method of obstetrics to give it its technical label. His patients are impressed by his warmth, his enthusiasm, his air of authority — and also with his accessibility. He has not taken advantage of his prestige; his current fees are exactly half the going rate for top specialists, and his office-home was inherited from his father, a well-known medical specialist.

He treats "ordinary cases." You do not have to be a movie star to get an appointment. His central principle is that women in labor must be given an active role in the births of their children, not treated as inanimate containers of babies.

He firmly believes that babies get off to a more favorable start if the mother has a drugless, i.e. unanesthetized, labor and delivery. Yet, as many of his patients attest, he is the center of activity at the birth, and a large percentage of "his women" have induced labors, which do involve drugs. Nor does his objection to drugs extend to pregnancy itself. Along with iron and vitamins, there are hormones to ensure a good beginning, drugs for the baby's teeth and brain, drugs to prevent early labor, to start labor at an optimal time, to soften the neck of the womb, etc.

American women who assume that "natural childbirth" means a minimum of medication from conception to delivery, that the parents and not the doctor are stage center at the birth, that the doctor is impersonal in his approach to a woman's body are startled. North American assumptions about "natural childbirth" do not match *accouchment sans douleur* in France.

Independent Researcher

The term has an old-fashioned ring to it, but this perfectly describes the researcher who visited Dr. Vellay – thanks to her mother's flower girl.

Independent researchers do not have institutional affiliations. They can also choose their projects free of funding considerations or institutional or corporate research priorities. These freedoms may give the researcher more room to consider her results without worry about the implications of her choices or research results for a funding entity or her employer.

The independent researcher is free of "publish or perish" considerations.

The independent researcher can work at her own pace. Aside from her obligation to observe the rules of her profession, she can combine her work with family obligations.

The independent researcher must be trained and experienced in research design and administration of that design. She must adhere to the ethics of her chosen profession to protect the rights of her human subjects. The research must be formal, the methods consistently applied.

She must be self-motivated and persistent. Even a small project can take two years from idea to writing a final report.

In the case of this researcher, the project – in varying forms – has occupied more than forty years.

The babies born to the researcher's interview subjects are now middle-aged. They no longer resemble the lively infants the researcher photographed with their mothers' permission in Paris in 1973-1975.

These babies and their mothers participated in a weekly play group and even at 3-6 months were interacting with each other far more than is usually understood.

But first – the interview protocol.

<u>Interview Protocol (Carbon Copy)</u>

                              Interview

<u>Background</u>
Name   Nationality   Fa's Name   Nationality
Address
Birthdate
Date of Marriage
Birthdates of children   Children's Place of birth

Mother: (Respondent's) Highest level of education obtained
   Type of work before and after marriage--and after birth of first child.
   If you have worked since your first child's birth, when did you go to work,
        full- or part-time? Childcare arrangements?
      Any thoughts on the problems of being a working mother?

Pregnancy:
   When in pregnancy did you confirm the pregnancy? Your reactions to being
        pregnant during the first trimester?
   How did you decide to go to Dr. Vellay?
      Schedule of visits?
      How would you describe your relationship with him during pre-natal visits?
         during labor? post-natal follow-up?
      How did you feel about the preparation classes? work with the sage femme?
      How was your general state of well-being during pregnancy? Any medical
          problems? family crises (whether related to pregnancy or not)? Other
          important occurences during pregnancy?
      Did you discern any personality differences between yourself pregnant and
         un-pregnant?

Childbirth:
   How did labor begin? How long did it last?
   Summary of progress of labor, including significant events, your reactions,
      any medical interventions (such as forceps, medication, etc.)
   What was the most useful to you in labor from your preparation? Anything not
      useful?
   Were there any pleasant or unpleasant surprises? If unpleasant, could they have
      been avoided, and if so, how?
   How did the staff relate to you during labor?
   Do you consider that you had a "successful" experience?

Baby:
   What were your immediate reactions to your baby? What were your early im-
      pressions of his/her character? Were these impressions accurate?
   How much contact--and of what kind--did you have with your baby in the 24 hours
      following birth? How do you feel about this?
   What is your baby's sex, birth weight, and health during the first 3 months?

Father's Role:
   His feelings about this pregnancy
   His participation in preparation and childbirth
   Does he feel he had a defined, useful role?
   His degree of involvement with the child? in child-care? entertainment of child?
         general interest?
   What effect, if any, has this childbirth experience had upon your marital rela-
      tionship?

Feeding of baby:
   Did you breast-or bottle-feed?
   Any pressure to do one or the other? If so, your reaction.
   If breast-feeding--when did you begin, how long did you continue, any special
      reason for stopping?
   What do you feel about which type of feeding is better for you?

17

Interview: page 2

Maternity Care facility:
  Name and type (clinic or hospital)
  Size of unit
  Length of your stay
  "Ambience"
  Attitude of staff
  How much contact did you have with your baby? Was there a central nursery?
  Did you get any rest?

Post-Natal:
  How long before you felt "back to normal"?
  Any complicating nuisances or difficulties?
  Household help, if any, when you returned home? for how long?
  Did you have a post-partum reaction?
      If so, what triggered it and how long after birth was it?
      What bothered you during the reaction?
      How long did it last?
      How did you come out of it?
    If no post-partum reaction, do you have any ideas as to how you
      avoided one?

Looking back on your pregnancy and childbirth experience:
  If you have had other children, what were the differences between this and
    other experiences?
  What would you do—or want to be—different next time?
  Do you have any unanswered questions about your pregnancy and labor?
      If so, what?

Finally, Is there anything you would like to add?
  What important issues have I missed?

Thank you!

The independent researcher can choose her own assistant. This one attracted
women in the parks who wanted to tell their childbirth stories.

The Women Who Told Their Stories
(Vellay and Non-Vellay Patients)

Amy had an unplanned pregnancy right out of college in New England. She looked for a doctor who would honor her preferences.

Andrea experienced pregnancy complications in France.

Ann was living in France and discovered that her husband would be transferred to Asia in the midst of her pregnancy, leaving her to care for their toddler alone for long stretches toward the end of her pregnancy.

Anna and Jose were from South America and recent arrivals in France for promised job and entrance into an academic program.

Barbara was a child of divorce whose husband was more interested in fatherhood than she was in motherhood, a US woman living in France with a French husband.

Britta had had a disappointing labor in Europe with her first child and was not happy with her pregnancy support during her second pregnancy.

Chris was a nurse pregnant with her first child.

Corinne, a nurse, experienced surprising emotional upheaval at the end of her pregnancy.

Cindy had witnessed a home birth that had scared her more than she realized.

Donna in France experienced severe complications during pregnancy and labor.

Drewe was not enthusiastic about having a child, but her husband wanted to be a father.

Eliane was a *lycée* teacher and felt that motherhood and elementary school teaching were a good fit.

Eva and her husband were PhD students who thought they could schedule parenthood according to the academic year.

Harriet had a child in the US under poor circumstances and a second in Finland which was more humane. She wanted to have a home birth for her third child in the United States.

Helene's husband took her on a tour of an obstetrical medical unit in France to reassure her, and it backfired.

This grad student expected to complete her thesis on time after her baby was born. She was lucky. Her baby took two long naps each day. She finished with time to spare.

Irene became pregnant a year after her three year-old daughter died of a sudden illness.

Isabel had had more children than she wanted and even in France lost her ability to work outside of the house.

Jeanne had her baby in a new French hospital with interesting architectural designed to enhance mother-baby contact.

Jennie was a New Yorker looking for family-centered childbirth culture in New York City.

Joy was a nurse who found pregnancy to be unexpectedly mysterious.

Karen had a confusing end to pregnancy.

Kathy had the type of birth she wanted in the United States.

Lorraine counted on her forceful personality to attain the care she wished in New York City.

Linda and David had been married for five years and had made four major moves in three countries during their marriage. She had earned a professional degree which she could not use in their current assignment. She had had previous medical complications.

Margaret was a university professor who experienced pregnancy complications in France.

Marianne was concerned about becoming a mother after growing up in a U.S. culture with strict role expectations for women.

Mary had given birth to a child both in the United States and in France.

Nancy published a book in France and became pregnant right afterwards.

Olga had two daughters and was married to a workaholic who spent too much time in a family business. She was Scandinavian and thought she might return to her home country with the children.

Patricia wanted her husband with her, but he was excluded and she was left alone for long periods during active labor and became demoralized. France experience.

Polly's husband had been delivered by Dr. Lamaze, and her mother-in-law encouraged her to engage Dr. Vellay for her pregnancies.

This woman had sat in the same position when interviewed at Dr. Vellay's maternity *clinique* the day after she gave birth. (No episiotomy.)

Rowena was a high fashion model in Paris.

Ruth was alone with her three year-old in France with her husband out of the country when she went into labor.

Sandy was working in France and was sole breadwinner. She was not covered under French social security health care and became acutely aware of how limited her US medical benefits were. She was experiencing significant conflicts with her obstetrician.

Sarah's husband traveled internationally often. She was unable to work due to her husband's irregular schedule and the need to provide consistent care for their young child.

Solange was a *lycée* teacher who anticipated little difficulty combining motherhood and her career in France.

Susan wanted her husband to be with her during labor and birth in France. He was excluded.

Sheila was an older mother from the Southern United States, and giving birth in the United States.

The researcher's copy of her report to Dr. Vellay was missing for years. The researcher discovered it in a neglected box in the bottom of a closet when doing some "cleaning out" on a rainy day. The report is a carbon that has withstood the test of time and survived multiple moves. Because of its detail and length, two findings are highlighted here.

Perhaps the most interesting finding is the number of Vellay patients with induced labors. This result directly contradicts Dr. Vellay's assertion during his childbirth education course that "I don't provoke births. I feel strongly about it."

Twelve of the 33 Vellay-attended childbirths in this survey were induced, which appears to be a practice method in conflict with his theories.

The second most important finding among Vellay patients included in this study was with breastfeeding. There appeared to be multiple examples of medical practice creating breastfeeding barriers.

Report to Dr. Vellay   [Notes prepared January 18, 1975 for in person meeting,]
From: Martha L. Deed, Ph.D.   Transcript: Original spelling, punctuation retained

Background: From August 1974 through January 1975, 23 women were interviewed. Nineteen (19) women were seen post-delivery only. Four (4) others were interviewed during pregnancy and afterwards. Each interview lasted a minimum of 90 minutes. Nine (9) women were interviewed more than once.

> Average age: 33
> Average number of children: 2 (Range: 1-4)

Interviews covered 46 children of whom 33 were delivered by women under care of Dr. Vellay. Of women who had non-Vellay deliveries, all of the most recent babies were Vellay babies. I.e. no woman had a baby elsewhere after having gone to Dr. Vellay.

All but one woman was able to speak English. However, several interviews were conducted almost entirely in French.

> Nationalities of patients:
> > 11 U.S.A.
> > 4 Scandinavian
> > 3 British Isles
> > 3 French
> > 1 each Canada, South America
>
> Referral Sources: (More than one source for several women)
> > 11   through friends
> > 6   recommended by other doctors
> > 3   through relatives treated by Dr. Vellay
> > 3   through Vellay's books and movies

Pregnancy stresses:

One of the most striking descriptive statistics of this group of women is that only three women experienced all of their pregnancies without either medical complications life threatening to the baby (i.e. disregarding annoyances such as fatigue, nausea, fainting) or the socio-economic and psychological stresses listed below.

Thus, in working with these women, it is important to realize that nearly all of them are anxious and psychologically vulnerable. Most are under considerable pressure and thus require particularly sensitive handling.

> Medical:
> > 10 -- Previous gynecological difficulty including absence of menses miscarriages, abortion, gynecological surgery, anatomical malformations, family history of difficult childbirth.
> > 7 -- Difficulty conceiving, taking 6 months to four years. Four women conceived only after hormone treatments.
> > 7 -- Difficult pregnancies, including at least one of the following:
> > > 3 staining first trimester, one of who was bedridden
> > > 1 threatened abortion
> > > 1 minor heart problem
> > > 4 threatened prematurity, three of whom were bedridden, the fourth treated by hormones alone. Two (2) women of this group had fragile premature babies.
> > 9 -- At least one unplanned pregnancy. Several within this group had seriously contemplated abortion.
>
> Psycho-socio-economic stresses
> > 5 -- marital problems (5 couples, all pregnancies of that marriage)
> > 5 -- economic problems (mother was the breadwinner, inadequate income or unemployed father)
> > 5 -- housing difficulties, including three who made international relocations during pregnancy

3 -- language problems severe enough to prevent meaningful communication in French during childbirth and leading to discomfort communicating in prenatal visits, inability to comprehend preparation classes
3 -- child's father opposed to pregnancy
2 -- mother's studies interrupted involuntarily
2 -- social isolation of mother (no friends, etc.)
2-- recent death within immediate family (parent, child)
1-- previous child with birth defects
1-- problem with husband's former wife
1-- forced to leave work due to pregnancy
1-- unmarried

Doctor-Patient Relationship: In analyzing responses to open-ended questioning (How would you describe your relationship with Dr. V and his medical care?), three basic, interrelated issues emerged: perceptions of Dr. V as a person, his competence and style of medicine, cultural factors.

A. Personality and General Attitude toward Patients: Twenty-two of the twenty-three women interviewd found him likeable, although a few had minor reservations. Frequently recurring descriptions were: warm, concerned, good personal relationship, honest and direct, doesn't keep you waiting, doesn't charge exhorbitant fees, childbirth is not a routine to him, is personally involved in preparation classes, "least male chauvinist pig doctor in Paris," respects difficulties of motherhood, and gives tactful advice about spacing along with contraceptive information, welcomes fathers and treats them well, alleviates fear.

Within this conext of overall approval, several women each were concerned with the following:
seems moody, irritable and rushed at times -- coinciding with difficulty in reaching him
for minor but troublesome symptoms needing treatment (e.g. hemorrhoids), but
also coinciding with his having to give a patient bad news (e.g. that she was dilating
early and would have to go to bed)
so confident that when things are going wrong he doesn't provide sufficient psychological support (Being unable to voice fears to the doctor increases anxiety.)
flirtatiousness--combined with the French custom of not using a sheet made many
Americans uneasy. Two were somewhat upset, a third felt "humiliated." Two others
frankly enjoyed the attention.
dogmatic, prima donna--"but he's entitled."
Several women found him quite frightening at the initial visit, primarily because of his
reputation as a doctor. All were put at ease by his friendliness.

B. Cultural factors: In the States and perhaps to a lesser extent in other places, natural or prepared childbirth refers not only to a method of childbirth but carries other assumpotions with it. Women do not realize these assumptions until faced with a doctor who practices the same method but with differences they did not expect in related aspects of care. Failure of either the woman or the doctor in being aware of these assumptions leads to confusion, misunderstanding, and can add to the psychological pressures of pregnacy. Unexpected experiences noted by several women each are listed below along with suggestions for the doctor who is relating to foreign patients in France.
No sheet. A minor factor but one which adds tension to the first examination. It might be useful to mention to the woman before she prepares for the physical exam that he knows she is used to a sheet, but it is not customary here. (It might also be useful to have one available in case a woman is shy.)

Uncertainty about the physician's role and lack of familiarity with midwives and *monatrices:* Like other American obstetrical patients, women seeking doctors who practice natural childbirth are used to being dependent on their *accoucheurs* both for medical care and emotional support. They expect to be seen monthly in the first seven months, then twice a month in the eighth month and weekly through the ninth month. They expect that the doctor is the one to deal with all fears and unusual sensations. Once labor begins, if he isn't present throughout, he is at least "in and out" during active labor and then present through the final dilation and delivery.

Thus, they need orientation to the French system where *monatrices* or midwives do much of the preparation for childbirth and answer questions. (In the States, for example, it is no use asking a nurse a medical question because her professional ethics do not allow her to answer it. She must refer the patient back to her doctor.

They also need clarification well ahead of time that the monatrice will guide them through labor and that the doctor arrives for the delivery phase only. (This is well-covered in the preparation classes, but some of the women most likely to misunderstand do not have sufficient French to attend the lectures.)

Use of medication. Much of the motivation for natural childbirth for most women is to avoid substances which might harm the baby during childbirth. This concern also carries over into the post-natal period and nursing afterwards. Women who have had natural childbirth previously outside of France have taken virtually no medication during their pregancies, sometimes not even patent drugs sold without a prescription. Most are very uneasy about medication, and no one who expressed this concern had brought it up with Dr. Vellay when he gave a prescription. Instead, they took the drug if they were desperate (e.g. afraid of miscarrying) and doing so added to their intense fears of having abnormal babies--or, they did not take the medication, and never told him. Careful explanations when drugs are prescribed might eliminate these anxieties, remembering that English-speaking women have probably encountered stories about thalidimide and reservations about other tranquilizers and sedatives, have read stories linking hormones to later genital defects in males and vaginal cancer in females. (They will not know which hormones are involved and will need to be reassured that what the doctor is giving is something different). If the woman has breastfed before (outside of France), the chances are good that this avoidance of medication will have continued throughout the nursing period, lest the chemical enter the baby through the milk and do harm. This confusion was best expressed by one woman who said, "If it is all right for the baby to get whatever I am taking while I am nursing, and it is all right for me to take drugs while I am pregnant--then why couldn't they give me something when it hurt?"
Note that none of the French women--or women who had lived for years in France before having their babies--were concerned about medication.

Breastfeeding. Without exception, the women going to Vellay desired to breastfeed their babies and assumed that this is part of natural childbirth. This issue is sufficiently complicated to be discussed in detail below. Hoever, as far as the cultural aspect goes, no woman was prepared to meet with any discouragement or difficulty with breastbeeding. All of the women were aware and pleased that Dr. V encourages breastfeeding. Given the difficulties of breastfeeding, however, several suggestions are made for pre-natal care:

Asking each woman how she plans to feed the baby.

If she wishes to breastfeed, providing her with an informative pamphlet, such as those put
out by La Leche League. (These are medically approved.)

Encourage breast preparation which can correct inverted nipples and toughen nipples. Even for women for whom such preparation isn't entirely necessary, it builds confidence by getting women used to handling their breasts.

Have names of women patients who have breastfed successfully and who are willing to talk with women considering breastfeeding.

Notify the *clinique* of women who wish to breastfeed.

Implementing these practices and others to be suggested below may help reduce the rate of failure in breastfeeding and make breastfeeding easier for those who do succeed.

C. Medical Factors

Nearly all of Dr. V's patients feel that he is unusually competent. Those who have criticism usually relate it to when he arrived at the birth rather than to any doubts arising during pre-natal care or to his behavior in the delivery room. This perception of competence in itself is highly reassuring to his patients. Competence is conveyed primarily through his handling of consultations, careful explanations (unless he is very rushed), and his preparation course.

Worries mentioned by several women included giving medication and [along with] breast-feeding (mentioned above), along with the following:

Induction--a highly complicated issue which will be dealt with only from the psychological point of view. Twelve (12) of the Vellay births were induced. Four of these were for medical reasons, e.g. small pelvis of the mother. The other eight (8) were for reasons of convenience (doctor going out of town, mother wanted to plan for the birth,etc.) or because of the mother's psychological condition.

Psychologically, induction raises several interesting issues. Several women were grateful for induction and felt relieved as a result. One woman had become severely depressed in late pregnancy over a death, and the baby's birth ended her grief. She was unable to request an induction, but very grateful for Dr. V's suggestion. Similarly, another woman who had been very late with her first labor appreciated a firm birth date.

Inductions occurring because of Dr. V's vacation schedule raised more conflict. The women involved were expecting to wait for spontaneous labor to begin and were not particularly uncomfortable. They experienced more anxiety before the inductions, feeling that it is awesome to know that "Tomorrow I will be a mother before noon." Anxiety with all women was increased if there were delays in giving medication once the scheduled time arrived.

Women who had inductions for medical reasons had no particular reaction to induction itself beyond wondering if their labors were rougher because of it. For them, the induction gave them the possibility of vaginal deliveries, and they were grateful.

In one case, the woman (French) did not realize that the birth was to be artificially provoked even though she was sent to the *clinique* and told she would have her baby "tomorrow." She resented not being asked directly for her opinion. Although against induction as "unnatural," she said she undoubtedly would have agreed anyway because "Dr. V is very persuasive." (She was one of the women induced because Dr. V was about to go on vacation.) A related issue here was that the *clinique* was very busy, several Vellay patients were delivering at once, she had no monitor, and she nearly delivered with only her husband in attendance.

From a psychological point of view, the following conclusions can be drawn: It can be assumed that the induction will raise anxiety about responsibility for the baby by specifying the date exactly. Women who are having extremely distressed pregnancies (e.g. psychologically upset or experiencing medical complications) are sufficiently relieved by an induction which puts a definite end to their worry that the offer of induction is greatly relieving. Once induction has been agreed to--and it is important that the women be clearly informed that induction is contemplated--it needs to proceed as smoothly as possible with medication or other procedures applied promptly, doctor and *monatrice* in active attendance, etc. since the labors are often rather rapid and chaotic. If induction is contemplated because of the doctor's schedule, it might be useful to give the woman a choice between induction now or the risk of having another doctor deliver. The results might still be the same (induction), but the women would have less conflict about it afterwards. For example, one woman who was induced is still worried that her baby wasn't ready to be born. Seven months later, she is attributing sleep difficulties and chronic diarrhea to the induction.

Difficult Pregnancies. It has been noted above that nearly all of the Vellay patients experienced significant difficulties during a pregnancy for which they were under V's care. Where the difficulties were marital, economic, or sociological, his approach was uniformly effective and most women felt that they had received excellent psychological support as well as medical care.

Particularly mentioned were his tact and sensitivity with a woman who had recently lost a young child. In this case, both parents saw him, and his support was invariably on the mark. The child Vellay delivered has been felt as a "second chance," and both parents frankly feel that the doctor's attitude toward them has been an important factor in the resolution of their grief at their child's death. In instances of unplanned children, even when abortion had been consisdered by the parents, Dr. V relates to patients in a manner which leaves the mother feeling "unguilty" about her abortion considerations. (The same applies to women who had actually had abortions.) It appears that his interest in the woman herself as an interesting person, not simply as a vessel for a fetus, is significant here. Where there is severe marital tension, Vellay is able to invite the fathers' involvement without increasing marital conflict. Furthermore, there appears to be no invitation to invite over-dependence in cases where the woman has no marital support.

Medical complications seem to call for varying approaches and several which occurred in several women will be discussed separately below.

Previous miscarriage or miscarriage. (8 women). Realistic assessments of the situation even though pessimistic at times are much-appreciated. One woman who did miscarry in the first trimester showed minimal sadness, saying V had told her that she might miscarry and had reassured her about her chances of having a successful delivery if she would wait several more months before trying to conceive again. Having warned the women initially, V also is good at reaassuring them once he feels the danger is past. Most of them do continue to worry to some extent about losing the baby, but their confidence in him is such that the worry is sporadic and fairly minimal. A specific measure which frankly upset one woman was listening to the fetal heartbeat very early in pregnancy when she might yet have miscarried. She reported that the FH made the baby very real to her; if she had then miscarried (she didn't), she would have been extremely upset.

Complications of late pregnancy. Here support seemed more problematic, partly, perhaps, because the baby was now very real to the mothers and loss at this stage would constitute a death. Measures necessary to prevent premature delivery are themselves extremely difficult psychologically. Interviews with three such women revealed that in each case the woman felt personally responsible for endangering her baby, citing such circumstances as overtiring themselves when realistically it appeared that they had done so no more than other women who were having normal pregnancies.

Being sent to bed and taking sedatives increased anxiety and guilt considerably. The long hours gave women too much time for painful rumination, and the effect of the drugs, while occasionally rendering the woman outwardly calm, was usually insufficient to calm her inwardly. Instead, two women reported that they lost control of their reasoning ability to the extent that they had intense panics, during which they could not reason themselves out of their fright.

At least three measures might significantly reduce the anxiety of women put on *maximum repos* or bedrest:

When the abnormality necessitating rest is discovered, the doctor needs to be sure he takes adequate time with the woman involved to explain exactly what her problem is, what he plans to do about it, what she needs to do about it. If she at first resists his insistence that she drop everything and go to bed, he should understand that the resistance undoubtedly is due to shock at the bad news -- not to her actual unwillingness to cooperate. Women who are told to go to bed, do in fact go to bed no matter how complicated their lives are and how responsible their jobs. If the doctor fails to acknowledge that of course it is difficult to get rid of one's responsibilities suddenly, the women are left feeling that he minimizes their importance at work, etc. This resentment makes tha doctor-patient relationship more complicated right at the time that complete understanding and trust are the most necessary.

If medications are to be taken, patients should be told of any potential for mood alterations and drowsiness. It would also be very useful to set up a telephone appointment about 5-7 days after beginning medication so that the patient and doctor can briefly discuss the impact, if any, of the medications. This would take little time, but would give the patient a sense of ongoing concern and care at a time when she badly needs it. Furthermore, it would serve as a check on those women who react abnormally to medication (either not getting enough effect or too much.)

If at all possible, arrangements should be made for seeveral consulatations with the *monatrice* at the patient's home. This would serve at least two purposes: 1) allay the patient's increased fears of delivery given the complication; 2) give the patient a chance to talk about her situation with someone medically knowledgable who could then report to the doctor.

A further possibility might be to have someone available who could visit bedridden women periodically to talk about their fears and experiences. A good listener would be essential, perhaps a mother who had similar experience, or a psychologist. In any case, the visitor should be briefed sufficiently that she wouldn't give unfoundeed reassurances.

Preparation Classes and Training by *Monatrices*. Nearly everyone who took the preparation classes felt they were excellent. All 23 women felt that they understood the physical side of their pregnancies and childbirths. There were few or no unansered questions about their labors and childbirths.

Those who had training by *monatrices* were nearly equally enthusiastic. They felt well-prepared for their own roles in giving birgh. The only reservations came from two women who had had previous births and felt that the *monatrices* were too dogmatic. Even so only one woman would have preferred not to have a *monatrice*, and those who had been unable to arrange for training regretted not having training.

Several specific suggestions were made:

It is essential to train for all births. A few women had been lazy about this and regretted it. They did not remember what to do and lacked the conditioned responses.

Training should start soon enough to be completed two or three weeks (at least) before the due date -- earlier if the woman delivered early previously. Women who had not completed training were somewhat anxious about what they had missed when they entered labor. Although the presence of the *monatrice* largely offset this anxiety, they would have done better to have completed training. As noted above, women who are having late pregnancy complications probably would benefit especially from training.

Several women felt that the question of pain should be dealt with more directly than is the case in either the class or by the *monatrices*. (I realize that this is a controversial issue.) A possible approach would be to state that no pain is the goal, that a significant percentage of women do experience childbirth with little or no pain. For the others, the techniques reduce pain to the point of bearable discomfort.

First-time parents, especially those newly-arrived to France who may have few friends with babies, are sorely in need of minimal baby care orientation. The one lecture available now does not appear to suffice. Along with information on feeding, elimination, sleeping habits, bathing, etc., parents could well use preparation for the adjustment necessary with a baby and some of the practical steps they can take to make early parenthood more fun and less anxioius. (Five of the 13 women having first babies under Vellay's care reported severe anxiety about the baby lasting six months or more. Others may have had lesser crises. I think that this proportion could be reduced considerably with childcare preparation.) In addition, three women remained depressed for six months or more over breastfeeding failures. (One woman wept as she told me about it a year later.) Two other women remain concerned that their babies are abnormal, among those giving birth for the first time. A total of 11 of the 13 women giving birth for the first time reported significant post-partmn stress related directly to childbirth itself or their new role as parents.

In contrast, only two of the 10 women who had given birth previously expressed such concerns. This difference points up the importance of additional orientation to actual parenthood for first-time parents now that the preparation for birth itself has been perfected.

A final suggestion is that several women felt that relaxation training could be improved. A number noted that relaxation training was at least as helpful after the birth as during it!

Other strongpoints:

Encouragement of husbands' attendance of classes.

Sufficient discussion of abnormal childbirths so that women who experienced them felt able to understand the situation and did not feel guilt about having an "unnatural" delivery. (I have found many women who feel guilty about their labors who have had cesarians, needed sedatives or lost control after being trained in other programs. Only one woman out of the 23 Vellay patients feels guilty about her labor, and she would have been relieved if she had had the chance to discuss it with Dr. V.)

Feelings about Labor and Delivery. As has been stated many times by people active in promoting psychoprophylactic childbirth, it is not sufficient to have a well-developed theory and good preparation for expectant parents. It is also necessary to have cooperative staff and a congenial facility. Among the 23 women interviewed, the following factors were frequently cited as being helpful during labor and delivery:

Good preparation and training (universally available to V patients)

Relationship of trust and confidence in a doctor and labor coach who are sincerely committed to ASD (available with few exceptions), both of whom are in attendance as arranged (see below)

Father's presence

Friendly, kind, competent staff (see below)

Attractive "normal" surroundings -- cheerful atmosphere, wearing own clothers, birds singing outside, food for father, etc.

Twelve of the 33 deliveries met all of these conditions. Numerous examples of unusually sensitive treatment were given and several are noted here to indicate the positive potentials of such care. In several instances care given was sufficient to offset labor stresses which existed at the onset of labor. (Number refers to patient code in case amplification is requested.)

7-- Difficult delivery during which parents and doctor appeared worried about outcome. When it was evident that all was well, doctor broke tension by teaching husband how to repair an episiotomy and had the husband handing him sutures. The couple still talk about this, for the husband was fascinated despite the fact that he is normally unable to stand the sight of blood.

10--Doctor intervened when coach and nurse were forcing woman to lie in an uncomfortable position. He placed her in a different position which brought immediate relief. She was impressed with his interest in her comfort. (The new position was less convenient for the nurses because of an IV.)

8--Patient's own doctor was out of town when she delivered. The replacement doctor was very supportive and was in and out of her room throughout a normal labor. He wasn't having to do much, but his presence was experienced as highly reassuring.

11-- Went into labor more than a month early and was terrified at the baby's condition. A nurse who sympathized with this woman's panic took her to visit an early baby who had just been born and was doing very well. This calmed the woman considerably and she proceeded to have an easier birth.

3--Very uneasy about the coming induction. She and her husband were both reassured by the gracious serving of *café au lait* and croissants on a silver service just before the induction along with the comment that the couple would almost surely have an equally pleasant lunch together with the baby beside them. (The bassinet was already in the room.)

17--Had a previous birth in New York which she found dehumanizing. She particularly enjoyed giving birth while wearing her husband's shirt and listening to the birds outside.

6, 23--Were both considerably upset because of recent severe disruptions in their lives. The nurses and everyone else were kind, reassuring and supportive, which helped the women to relax. When complications arose in both cases during advanced labor or delivery of the placenta, staff appeared calm and the parents were able to remain calm as well.

18--Went into labor while her husband was in the States. Everyone was very sympathetic and gave her considerable support until he could arrive.

Stresses and Delivery. Unfortunately, such support as given above cannot be relied upon, particularly during crowded times at the *clinique*. Lapses in some cases were perceived by patients as indicating lack of awareness of their physical condition. At other times, patients felt that staff were sadistic or simply insensitive. Women who felt that they were treated badly (in terms of psychological support) by the nursing staff all noted that staff attitude took a dramatic turn for the better once the doctor arrived. Thus, these lapses will be noted specifically.

Absence or lateness of attending doctor. This situation invariably presents difficulties for the patient, but the difficulty can be surmounted by notifying the patient immediately that the doctor is out-of-town and that Dr. So-and-so will deliver instead. When Dr. V was out-of-town, the situation was well-handled. The fact that the patients involved (3) were satisfied with the way things were handled after being initially upset is an indication of the support given. In another case, Dr. V arrived when the staff expected him, but the parents, newly arrived in France, were upset because they had assumed he would come earlier. It was a misunderstanding.

Seven women had childbirths which they described as harrowing due to a combination of factors (known and unknown) culminating in Dr. V's absence or lateness at the delivery. Most of them feel that Dr. V was as much a victim of circumstances as they were and do not blame him. Nonetheless, all seven were traumatized by their childbirth experiences. This situation emerged as one which should receive high priority for prevention, especially because other women have such good memories of their childbirth experiences.

3, 9, 19--were having induced labors. Two of them were induced because Dr. V was going away; the third had requested the induction for her own convenience. The women had had previous rapid spontaneous delivery and told the *monatrice* and nurses. In all three cases, the women are convinced that if V hadn't actually been in the *clinique* at the time, he would have missed the delivery entirely because the nurses did not heed their past history or call V on their own. V came into the toom to examine #3 on his own initiative (without having been summoned by the staff) upon arrival at the *clinique* and discovered that delivery was imminent. He was scheduled to deliver someone else but found he needed to stay and deliver her first. Patient #9's husband was alone with her when the couple realized that the baby was the the perineum. He ran from the room and managed to find V who delivered the baby. #19's labor was unexpectedly rapid and again there was a frantic last minute search, which left the woman and her husband feeling very resentful.

14, 22--were both in the *clinique* under observation because they were threatening to go into premature labor. In both cases, the women began having regular contractions and reported this as soon as regularity was established, in each case several hours before the eventual births. Neither felt that the staff took any notice of them. One woman reported strong pressure on her rectum and was given a bedpan by a passing nurse. Suddenly, she had a strange sensation. Her husband looked and saw the baby's head. A midwife delivered the baby. The other woman was unattended. She eventually panicked and began screaming. Another doctor in the *clinique* delivered the baby. Both babies were born with severe complications, and one mother had severe complications as well. They feel they were not adequately observed in the *clinique*, that no one realized what was happening and therefore no one called Dr. V in time.

12, 20--both were having normal, but very rapid labors. Both women know that staff failed to notify Dr. V quickly enough because staff were fighting about it in front of them. In each case, the *monatrice* arrived to find that no one had called Vellay or his replacement and began scolding *clinique* staff as they struggled to hold the baby back until a doctor arrived. Patient 20 had this situation occur with both deliveries, once when Vellay was out of town--which confirms her feeling is that the problem is with the *clinique* itself and not with the doctors who use it. For these women, having the baby held back was a thoroughly painful and upsetting experience, and they wonder yet if their babies were damaged by this practice.

Staff disputes were cited by 8 women as being quite unsettling. In several instances (as noted above) the disputes seemed necessry to bring about appropriate action, e.g. notifiying the doctor of an imminent birth. It appears that women in labor are quite sensitive to disharmony around them, probably because labor is experienced as a very challenging experience which requires all of their emotional as well as physical resources. It would be helpful if such arguments could take place out of patients' presence.

Poor relationship between Couple and Staff affected childbirth experiences of eight women. These incidents occurred only in the doctor's absence. Although no incident noted here affected the physical aspects of birth, all were emotionally influenced. As one woman said, "I had no joy in the birth because everyone was so mean." Again, it seems good to mention specifics in case a pattern is revealed:

11--was kept waiting in the reception area for more than an hour when she was having frequent, strong contractions. Once settled, the *monatrice* arrived and began scolding her for being frightened. She later lost control entirely (the only one in the sample to do so under ordinary circumstances.) Afterwards, she felt very guilty about this and wanted to talk to Dr. V about it, but felt he didn't want to hear about it. Her next child was born a month early. This time a nurse teased her for being frightened.

12--*clinique's* midwife was very rough with her and made an unnecessarily rough examination, apparently out of bad temper.

14--nurse told her it wasn't important for her to have clothes for her baby if it was born early because "These babies have problems; they die."

19--nurse interfered with woman's breathing techniques, although the woman was finding them effective at the time, telling her she should do something else. She refused to let the woman breathe as she needed to as long as she was in the room. Pain and increased tension were the result.

16--*monatrice* interfered with the couple's relationship and with the woman's technique by imposing methods which the woman did not like. This couple had had a child together previously, and the father had coached the woman successfully. The *monatrice* withdrew to one side but appeared resentful; mother felt the *monatrice* was wishing pain on her.

20--received a very painful shave from a rough nurse who cursed at her when the woman objected. Later she was in attendance with the *monatrice*, who scolded the nurse for not calling Dr. V, and the nurse in turn was screaming at the woman not to push, with the *monatrice* defending the patient.

Other stresses: Cesarian was being considered in the cases of two women with very inefficient labor, fathers were unavoidably late at two other deliveries, and one *monatrice* was unavoidably absent. Two women were told to go home when Vellay had told them to stay. Both did give birth within several hours.

Summary: Seven (7) of the 13 women having first deliveries experienced stress, and 11 of the 19 women delivering subsequent babies experienced stress. (In this case, the total is more than 23 because 9 women had both their first and subsequent children under V's care.) Stress is defined as a medical complication (prematurity, arrested labor, bleeding, poor presentation) or failure of psychological support.

Experiences and Feelings about the *Clinique* after Childbirth.

3 women--satisfied with no reservations.

4 women-- satisfied with their own care and care of their own babies, but feel *clinique* is seriously deficient in adequate nursing care and facilities for emergencies. One of the four was left unobserved after a D and C for 24 hours and described herself as "terrified." Her comment: "I don't understand how Dr. Vellay puts up with it."

16 women-- felt that their own care was very deficient. In instances where Dr. Vellay was informed (6 instances) care was dramatically improved during the current confinement (5 instances) or the next (1).

A fair summary of the women's view is that they like Dr. Vellay well enough to tolerate the *clinique*, especially if he can be requested to intervene ahead of time. However, all but three women feel they are taking a risk in using the *clinique*. The risk is mostly to the baby, but there is also some risk to themselves. Thus, only three women of the 23 interviewed feel comfortable in using the *clinique*. Others, who enjoy the luxurious atmosphere, good meals, etc. range from complaining that the medical care is not as good as the hotel services to those who feel guilty that they enjoy staying in a place at the expense of really excellent care for their babies.

Breastfeeding complaints, given Dr. Vellay's unquestioned positive attitude toward breastfeeding, occurred almost universally. Seventeen (17) women reported that their efforts to breastfeed were actively interfered with. Reported incidents occurred with such frequency and similarity among these 17 women that one is forced to conclude that the nursing staff at the *clinique* is generally opposed to breastfeeding for reasons that are not readily apparent. Each of the following negative approaches was reported by several women:

Baby was not brought for feedings until second or third day.

"Your breasts are too small."

"Your milk is not good for the baby."

Nursing baby roughly pulled off breast by a nurse who said the baby had had enough and should be back in bed.

Babies given supplementary bottles at night against orders--sometimes given supplements in front the the mothers during the day.

Mother threatened that baby would be given supplements if baby drank as little as 5 cc's too little milk at a single feeding.

"You can't nurse if you work."

"Your baby is too little to nurse."

"Your baby is too big to nurse."

Weighing baby before and after each nursing accompanying negative remarks about how poorly baby is doing.

"The baby prefers his formula to your milk."

Given an injection to stop milk production when she had said she wanted to nurse. (Only happened to one woman.)

"You have to stop nursing if you are engorged."

"You have to stop nursing if you have sore nipples."

"You have to stop nursing if you are temporarily sick."

All 23 women wanted to breastfeel Eleven (11) women were able to breastfeed at least one baby without regular supplements for at least two months.

Of the 17 women who were discouraged from breastfeeding by the nurses,

5 appealed to Dr. Vellay for help and all breastfed successfully.

2 had friends who had successfully nursed and who helped and succeeded.

1 had an interested pediatrician and succeeded.

2 had underweight babies, ignored discouraging advice and went on to nurse for 6 months with excellent results for the babies.

1 who had nursed previously succeeded.

5 women having their first babies who had no other help with breastfeeding failed and were significantly upset by the failure.

1 woman who had nursed successfully previously in another hospital was unable to nurse her baby born in the *clinique.*

Suggestions (in addition to those given above under pre-natal care):

Re-examination of such practices as weighing before and after each nursing. Many pediatricians consider this practice unnecessary and it definitely unnerves the mothers. Where weighing is necessary, it should be done out of the mother's sight and the results given only by someone sympathetic to breastfeeding.

More basically, an inquiry in the why's of all this negative reaction from the staff.

> Dr. V could encourage his patients who have expressed a desire to breastfeed to let him know of any incidents so he can counteract negative (and often erroneous) information.

> Presenting mothers with the possibility of caring for their babies in their rooms on a 24-hour basis in order to establish frequent breastfeeding on demand and to avoid staff interference. (The problem here, of course, is that the mother gets less rest. However, if she is very upset, e.g. over nursing conflicts, she doesn't rest any way.)

Note: A Paris pediatrician with many successfully breastfeeding mothers notes that the *clinique* stays are so long (at least a week) that if trouble over breastfeeding develops in the *clinique* it is too late to reverse the process by the time the women and their babies are discharged.

A final suggestion: In the absence of any other changes, breastfeeding success can be improved simply by having an experienced nursing mother visit the *clinique* or maintain telephone contact, sharing her own experiences, making books available, etc.

Baby care difficulties. As noted earlier, it is a problem, particularly for first-time mothers that they have very little experience in baby care before getting home with the baby. Once they feel rested, it would help to encourage them to do some sponging, changing, etc. of the baby so they can gain confidence while still in the *clinique* where they can ask questions of Dr. V or a pediatrician.

Mothers particularly appreciated having the babies with them from the beginning, especially women who had experienced separation from previous babies. However, some women felt (and one was) forgotten by the staff and were given what they considered to be inadequate medical coverage for the baby:

> An rh-reaction was missed until the baby was several days old and very ill.

> One baby was released from the clinique with untreated bronchitis.

> Another baby became ill with diarrhea and went untreated for several days (by which time the child was very ill).

> Two babies were released from the *clinique* with undiagnosed, and hence untreated, mouth infections.

> Three mothers felt that their babies were very roughly handled.

> A several hour delay occured in examining a weak premature baby and moving him to a treatment center.

Mothers' care difficulties. Most of the mothers enjoyed their *clinique* stays, feeling that the food was excellent the "rules" minimal and the surroundings pleasant. They especially liked the freedom given to fathers to come and go as they pleased, take meals together, etc. One woman was left completely untended for the first 24 hours following delivery because no one knew she was there. Another became ill and had to wait 48 hours for any treatment, and a third found her stay exhausting because she was waked up so frequently by staff. However, in general the treatment given to mothers was the most satisfactory aspect of their stay--with the exception of advice concerning breastfeeding.

Responses to ASD. All 23 women endorse this method. None, even those who had difficult experiences would prefer a sedated or anesthetized birth. All of those planning future births would use the method again. As noted earlier, 5 women feel the name is wrong and that the issue of pain should be faced more directly. These five women felt they had been "tricked" in this one respect.

> Motives for choosing ASD:
>> Desire to take an active role in the birth process
>> Avoidance of anesthesia
>> Desire to be awake and in control of oneself
>> Desire to make birth an experience which fathers can share.

Desire for a practical, safe method of handling pain.

It should be further noted that several women were completely unaware of having made a choice of childbirth method. One woman was a second generation ASD mother; her husband was a "Lamaze baby." Other women have heard so much about ASD that they simply assume this is the way everyone has their babies. Thus, it appears that one of the goals set by Vellay in <u>Painless Childbirth</u> (Hutchinson with Allen and Unwin, 1959) is beginning to be realized.

Notes on Fathers' Role: The extent of the fathers' involvement with the mothers' pregnancies and child-births was striking in comparison with experiences of 26 women who were not Vellay patients:
14 of 23 Vellay fathers attended preparation classes with the women
 3 of 26 non-Vellay fa's   "   "   "   "   "   "
 7 Vellay fa's accompanied their wives to at least one doctor's appointment
 2 Non-Vellay fa's   "   "   "   "   "   "   "   "   "
23 Vellay fathers were present for labor and delivery
14 Non-Vellay fa's saw their children born.

Thus it seems indisputable that the ASD approach does encourage fathers to take a more active role.

A further issue is the quality of fathers' participation. Twenty-two (22) of the 23 Vellay patients positively appreciated their husbands' presence. One (who is one of the five with marital difficulties) was annoyed and hampered because her husband brought friends with him and they joked on one side of the room while she tried to deal with her labor on the other. She experienced this as emotional desertion. In the other four instances of marital difficulty, it appeared that the husbands were helpful at the time of the birth. Although problems recurred afterwards, the births are remembered as times of cooperation.

Many husbands, according to their wives, felt unneeded at the births even though their wives were glad to have them there. Giving "moral support" does not appear to be a sufficient role for husbands who welcome involvement. Where husbands performed other functions as well, massage, help with relaxation and breathing, interpreting (for non-French-speaking women), timed contractions, etc. they invariably felt necessary to their wives at the births.

If husbands could be encouraged to attend at least some of the sessions their wives have with the *monatrices*, they could take more responsibility.

Several women mentioned that the *monatrice* was necessary to keep a strict, working atmo-sphere and that their husbands would not be capable of this. Such reasoning may be the other side of the husbands' feelings of uselessness. It is a similar argument to the one used to bar husbands from the labor or delivery room. (They'd faint, etc.) Such reasoning has a destructive effect on a man's sense of competence to the extent that he agrees. He cannot take the place of an experienced *monatrice* any more that he would wish to deliver the baby himself, but there could be more responsibility for him without supplanting the *monatrice*.

One woman warned that couples should not have the importance of the birth for the couple be over-emphasized, lest something go wrong and prevent his attendance. This can be accomplished with the same apporach used to tell women about the occasional necessity for surgery; it's unfortunate, but the training is still useful.

One of the reasons given for involving fathers more in the birth process is that this may lead to greater participation in the care of the child afterwards. As measured by actual childcare activities, there was no appreciable difference between the Vellay and non-Vellay fathers. About half the fathers, feed, bathe, and change their babies as well as the mothers. In eight families, four from each group, the parents have had 50-50 responsibility for an appreciable length of time (a month or more) without apparent ill effects. Only a small minority of fathers -- 7 in the Vellay group and 4 in the non-Vellay group -- have roles which are restricted to occasional playing with their children.

Rating the emotional involvement of fathers with their children is, of course, a much more complicated matter, and many women's impression is that being at the birth increased their husbands' feeling for these children greatly. This seems to be the most noticeable (again, an impression) among couples where the father had previously been barred from the birth or where the couples have made a point of finding care that permits the fathers' presence. With other couples, the father's presence may be taken for granted and nothing special is noted.

In conclusion, while one would not argue that the Vellay fathers are more involved than other fathers with their children, one can state with some confidence that their fairly high rate of involvement seems part of a wider trend for fathers to take a greater role in the care of their children.

--00--

About the Author

Martha Deed, PhD is a psychologist whose research in domestic violence, child custody and patients' rights has been funded by the Violence Against Women Act, The Baldy Center at the University of New York at Buffalo, and the New York State Bar Association. As an independent researcher in the 1970s, Dr. Deed spent more than two years in Paris where she met Dr. Pierre Vellay, a leading proponent of the Lamaze method of *accouchement sans douleur* (painless childbirth). She attended Dr. Vellay's childbirth education classses and interviewed 23 of his patients, accounting for 33 Vellay births. In addition, she interviewed more than 20 non-Vellay patients. Births took place in Europe and in North and South America.

Dr. Deed served on the American Psychological Association's Advisory Board for the Presidential Task Force on Family Violence, and more recently on the National Quality Forum's Patient Safety Committee. She is a past President of the Clinical Division, New York State Psychological Association and a past member of New York State Surrogate Court's Medical Decision Making Committee and New York State's Department of Health Medical Records Access Committee.

When not functioning as a patient advocate, Dr. Deed is a poet. She has published a collection, Climate Change (FootHills Publishing, 2014) and numerous chapbooks, most recently "We Should Have Seen This Coming" (locofo chaps, 2017). Her mixed-genre examination of her daughter's death from medical mistake, The Last Collaboration (Furtherfield, and Friends of Spork, 2012), combines her work as a poet and researcher.

Birth: Where Culture and Medicine Meet, and Culture Shock: Pregnancy, Childbirth and Early Parenthood At Home and Abroad in the 1970s augment Deed's professional publications on her childbirth research and are intended for the general reader.

Birth recounts the origins of the childbirth research and contains Deed's extensive report to Dr. Vellay based upon her interviews.

Culture Shock tells the stories of more than 50 women (including the 23 Vellay mothers) whom Deed interviewed throughout their pregnancies and early months of parenthood.

www.ingramcontent.com/pod-product-compliance
Lightning Source LLC
Chambersburg PA
CBHW051133250726
48655CB00007B/3031